Better Rebidding with Bergen

By Marty Bergen

Bergen Books

Thanks To:

Layout, cover design, and editing by
Hammond Graphics.

My very special thanks to: Ollie Burno, Caitlin,
Cheryl Angel, Cheryl Bergen, Gary Blaiss,
Larry Cohen, Nancy Deal, Ned Downey,
Pete Filandro, Jim Garnher, Terry Gerber,
Lynn and Steve Gerhard, Pat Harrington, Steve Jones,
Doris Katz, Al Kimel, Harriet and David Morris,
Phyllis Nicholson, Mary and Richard Oshlag,
Helene Pittler, David Pollard, Mark Raphaelson,
Jesse Reisman, John Rudy, Maggie Sparrow,
Tom Spector, Merle Stetser, Fred Stewart,
and Bobby Stinebaugh.

Bergen Books
9 River Chase Terrace
Palm Beach Gardens, FL 33418-6817

First Edition published 2003.
Printed in the United States of America.
10 9 8 7 6 5 4 3 2

First Printing: April, 2003
Second Printing: July, 2007

Library of Congress Control Number: 2003091159

ISBN 0-9716636-6-1

♠ ♡ **Caribbean Bridge Cruises** ◇ ♣
with Marty Bergen and Larry Cohen
All cruises depart and return to Ft. Lauderdale, Florida.
For prices, itinerary, flyers and other info, or to be on the
mailing list for future cruises with Marty and Larry, call:
Bruce Travel 1-800-367-9980
To participate in bridge activities,
you must book the cruise with Bruce Travel.

These cruises feature daily lectures, as much duplicate bridge as
you care to play, plus all the activities, entertainment and
ambiance that you'd expect to find on a first-class cruise ship.

2007 Cruise with National Champion Larry Cohen
Sunday, Nov 4 - Sunday, Nov 11   Ports include: Bahamas,
St. Thomas, Virgin Islands, Grand Turk, Road Town Tortola,
Half Moon Cay, and Turks & Caicos Islands.

2008 Cruise with National Champion Marty Bergen
Popular lecturer/teacher, author of 19 books and ten-time
National Champion Marty Bergen's next cruise will take place
Sunday Nov 16-Sunday Nov 23, 2008. Ports include: Bahamas,
Mexico, Costa Maya, Grand Cayman, Turks & Caicos Islands,
Half Moon Cay, and Grand Turk. Highlights include: daily
lessons featuring brand-new material with a dynamic approach.

• Free private lesson for groups of 5 signing up together •
• Free drawing to play duplicate on cruise with Marty •
• Free Bergen book for those signing up early •

**For info on books or CDs
with GREAT DISCOUNTS,
please refer to pages 70-72.**

To order, call **1-800-386-7432**
or email: mbergen@mindspring.com

Bridge Books by Marty Bergen

Bergen for the Defense

Declarer Play the Bergen Way

More Declarer Play the Bergen Way

Marty Sez...

Marty Sez...Vol 2

Marty Sez...Vol 3

Points Schmoints!

More Points Schmoints!

Bergen's Best Bridge Tips

Understanding 1NT Forcing

To Open or Not to Open

Hand Evaluation: Points Schmoints!

Bergen's Best Bridge Quizzes, Vol. 1

Negative Doubles

Introduction to Negative Doubles

Better Bidding with Bergen, Vol I

Better Bidding with Bergen, Vol II

Contents

Stop – Read This 6

Opener's Rebid Guidelines 7-11

All About Reverses 12-14

Chapter 1: 1♣ – 1♢ 15

Chapter 2: 1♣ – 1♡ 21

Chapter 3: 1♢ – 1♡ 27

Chapter 4: 1♣ – 1♠ 33

Chapter 5: 1♢ – 1♠ 39

Chapter 6: 1♡ – 1♠ 45

Chapter 7: 1♣ – 1NT 51

Chapter 8: 1♢ – 1NT 55

Chapter 9: 1♡ – 1NT 59

Chapter 10: 1♠ – 1NT 63

After Opening in 3rd & 4th Seat 67

Advanced Rebids 68-69

Highly Recommended

Books and CDs 70-72

Stop — Read This

This book focuses on opener's second bid after partner's 1-level response. The opponents have passed throughout. The examples were carefully chosen to apply to the great majority of players, regardless of their conventions or the form of scoring.

In this book, it does not matter if you do, or do not play:

- In response to 1♣: "up the line" or usually bypass diamonds to show major ASAP (the latter is my decided preference)
- Strong jump-shifts or weak jump-shifts
- 1NT Forcing
- 2/1 Game-Forcing
- Jacoby 2NT
- Inverted Minors
- etc etc.

Keep in mind:

Opening Bids:
Based on the Rule of 20.
Five-card majors.
Opening 1NT = 15-17 HCP.
Opening 2NT = 20-21 HCP.

Quick Tricks – AK = 2, AQ = 1½, A = 1, KQ = 1, Kx =½

Tenace – A combination of non-consecutive honors.
Some examples are AQ and KJ.

Guidelines for Opener's Second Bid
after a 1-level response in a suit

This section describes the requirements for selecting an appropriate rebid. Recommended length, strength, distribution, and other relevant information for each rebid is provided, along with a typical example.

1♡ or 1♠ (new suit at 1 level)
Fewer than 19 HCP
Not forcing
4-card suit (if 5 cards, then 6 in suit opened)
Never 4-3-3-3 distribution

After 1♣ – 1♢
Bid 1♠ with:
♠ A J 9 7   ♡ 7 4   ♢ A 7   ♣ K Q 8 6 3

1NT
Fewer than 15 HCP
Not forcing
Balanced distribution after a 1♢ or 1♡ response
May not be balanced after a 1♠ response
Does not promise stoppers in unbid suits

After 1♣ – 1♢
Bid 1NT with:
♠ A Q 4   ♡ K 10 4   ♢ 9 8 2   ♣ K 9 5 3

Rebidding original suit at 2 level
Fewer than 16 HCP
Not forcing
6-card suit (7 is rare)
Usually a minimum opening bid

After 1♣ – 1◇
Bid 2♣ with:
♠ A 9   ♡ 7 3   ◇ Q 5 4   ♣ K Q J 7 4 3

2 of new suit
(lower-ranking than opener's first suit)
Fewer than 19 HCP
Not forcing
4-card suit (could be 5)
Never a balanced hand

After 1◇ – 1♠
Bid 2♣ with:
♠ A 3   ♡ 7 4   ◇ K Q 10 9 2   ♣ A 8 7 3

Raise to 2 of responder's suit
Fewer than 15 HCP
Not forcing
Usually 4-card support, but might be 3-card support

After 1◇ – 1♠
Bid 2♠ with:
♠ K J 5 3   ♡ A 6 2   ◇ A 10 9 2   ♣ J 3

Reverse (nonjump)
2 of new suit (higher-ranking than opener's first suit)
17+ HCP (might be fewer with great distribution)
Forcing for one round
4-card suit (if 5 cards, then 6 in suit opened; 3 cards rare)
Original suit is longer than second suit

After 1♢ – 1♠
Bid 2♡ with:
♠ K J   ♡ A Q 9 6   ♢ A K J 10 5   ♣ 6 3

Jump-Shift (single jump to 2 or 3 level)
19+ HCP (might be fewer with upgradable hand)
Game-forcing
4-card suit (could be 5 cards; 3 cards rare)
Usually an unbalanced hand with 5+ cards in original suit

After 1♢ – 1♡
Bid 2♠ with:
♠ K Q 10 8   ♡ A   ♢ A K 9 4 2   ♣ A 8 5
Bid 3♣ with:
♠ K Q   ♡ 8   ♢ A K J 7 4   ♣ A Q 10 4 2

2NT
18-19 HCP (might be fewer with upgradable hand)
Invitational, but rarely passed
Usually balanced
Usually contains stoppers in both unbid suits

After 1♣ – 1♡
Bid 2NT with:
♠ A Q 7   ♡ Q 10   ♢ A K J   ♣ Q 9 8 5 4

Jump to 3 in suit opened

More than a minimum opening bid
Invitational
6+ cards with strong suit
Denies a 4-card major

After 1♣ – 1♡
Bid 3♣ with:
♠ 9 3   ♡ K Q   ◇ K 3 2   ♣ A K J 10 5 3

Jump Raise to 3 level

16+ to 19- distribution points in support of partner's suit
Invitational
4-card support

After 1♣ – 1♠
Bid 3♠ with:
♠ Q J 7 6   ♡ A   ◇ K Q 7   ♣ K 9 7 6 4

3NT (alertable)

Enough playing strength to bid game
A strong suit of at least 6 cards
Invites slam
1-2 cards in responder's suit
Stoppers in unbid suits (almost always)

After 1♣ – 1♠
Bid 3NT with:
♠ 8   ♡ A 7 6   ◇ K J   ♣ A K Q 9 8 5 3

Splinter Raise (artificial, double jump)
A singleton or void in suit bid
At least 19 distribution points in support of responder's suit
Invites slam
4-card support
At 3-level, alertable now; at 4-level, explain after auction

After 1♡ – 1♠
Bid 4♣ with:
♠ K Q J 2   ♡ A 10 8 6 4   ◇ A K J   ♣ J

Jump to 4 in original major
Too many HCP to open four, but not enough to open 2♣
A strong suit, usually with 7-8 cards

After 1♡ – 1♠
Bid 4♡ with:
♠ K Q 8   ♡ A Q J 9 6 5 4 2   ◇ 8   ♣ 7

Jump Raise to 4 level
At least 19 distribution points in support of responder's suit
Invites slam
4-card support
If playing splinter bids, usually no short suit

After 1♡ – 1♠
Bid 4♠ with:
♠ A K 9 5   ♡ A K 10 7 5   ◇ A 3   ♣ 6 2

Opener Reverses
(after a 1-level response)

How can you identify opener's reverse? At his second turn, he bids a new suit at the two level without jumping. The new suit must be higher-ranking than the suit opened.

What does opener show? He promises an unbalanced hand with 17+ HCP (or a bit less with great distribution). His first suit is always longer than the second.

Why are reverses necessary? When opener has a strong hand but is unsure about the best contract, he needs an economical, forcing bid which indicates strength, but also preserves all options.

After 1♢ – 1♠
???

♠ Q 9 4 ♡ A K J 2 ♢ A K 8 6 4 ♣ 4

♠ K ♡ K Q J 9 ♢ A Q 9 7 6 4 ♣ K 2

♠ 7 2 ♡ A K 2 ♢ A K Q 9 7 4 3 ♣ 5

These are very different hands; but on all three, opener should reverse by bidding 2♡, and await developments. If 2♡ was not available as a forcing bid, opener would be poorly placed.

What's the problem? Because opener did not jump, many players forget that opener is showing a big hand. Also, opener's reverse is forcing, *but not forcing to game,* so we don't know where we stand. If responder is weak, how can he tell opener that they *may* need to stop below game? It's safe to say that no other topic results in so much confusion.

Regrettable Reverse Ramifications

Because opener needs 17 HCP to reverse, sometimes, he should "break the rules" to avoid reversing with less than adequate values.

Therefore, at his first turn, he might open:

1. 1NT with two doubletons.
♠ K 5   ♡ A Q 8 5   ◇ Q J 9 8 3   ♣ K 10

2. 1◇ with four diamonds and five clubs.
♠ 8 5   ♡ 9 3   ◇ A K J 9   ♣ A 8 6 4 3

3. A 5-card suit, despite a lower-ranking 6-card suit.
♠ Q 7   ♡ A J 9 5 3   ◇ K Q 7 6 4 3   ♣ —

On other hands, opener has no option at his first turn. He must then be very careful in selecting his rebid, to avoid reversing with a minimum opening bid.

After   1◇ – 1♠
???

Each of the following hands is not strong enough for a 2♡ reverse; therefore, opener should bid:

1NT with   ♠ 3   ♡ K Q 9 7   ◇ K J 6 5 3   ♣ K 10 9

2♣ with   ♠ —   ♡ A J 10 3   ◇ A Q 9 5 2   ♣ 5 4 3 2

2◇ with   ♠ 7   ♡ A Q J 8   ◇ J 8 7 5 4 2   ♣ K Q

2♠ with   ♠ 4 3 2   ♡ A K J 6   ◇ A 8 5 4 3   ♣ 3

Using a Notrump Bid to Avoid a Reverse

Even when strong enough to reverse, I often prefer not to.

After 1♣ – 1♥, a 2♦ reverse is the textbook bid with:

    ♠ K J   ♡ K 4   ♢ K 6 5 3   ♣ A K J 5 3
    ♠ A Q J   ♡ K   ♢ Q J 8 4   ♣ K Q 7 5 3

But, I would rebid 2NT with each hand. Why?

2NT is specific; 18-19 HCP. Opener is inviting game, but responder is free to pass. If responder elects to bid, we are definitely going to game. Very precise. Both players know exactly where they stand.

2♦ would promise 17 HCP, but *might* be as many as 21. Responder must bid again, even with garbage. Opener *might* intend to force to game, but then again, he *might not*.

Similarly, as dealer, I would open an imperfect 2NT with:

    ♠ A Q   ♡ K J 10 4   ♢ A K J 5 2   ♣ Q 9

If you open 1♢ and get the likely 1♠ response, your 2♥ reverse will send you to the fuzzy-wuzzy world of "after reversing, what the heck do we do now?" No thank you!

In conclusion:
1. Don't reverse with a minimum opening bid. You may need to look ahead when selecting your opening bid; on other hands, choose your rebid discreetly.
2. Responder must be able to recognize opener's reverse.
3. Your partnership must practice reverse auctions, and decide what happens "after the reverse."
4. When practical, avoid reverse auctions (even with a strong hand) by making a notrump bid.
5. *It's not unreasonable....* Before going to play bridge, say a little prayer: "please, please, no reverses today!"

Chapter 1

Opener Rebids after 1♣ – 1♦

For each of these hands, what should opener bid now?

1. ♠ K Q 9 ♡ A J 7 5 ♢ Q ♣ A Q 6 5 3

2. ♠ A K Q J ♡ 5 4 3 2 ♢ — ♣ Q J 9 8 4

3. ♠ Q 7 5 2 ♡ K J 3 ♢ A 9 8 ♣ Q J 4

4. ♠ Q 2 ♡ 8 7 4 3 ♢ A ♣ K Q J 10 8 6

5. ♠ 5 2 ♡ K 7 3 ♢ A K J ♣ Q 8 7 5 2

6. ♠ 4 ♡ A K J ♢ J 4 3 ♣ A K Q J 10 3

7. ♠ A K 8 6 ♡ 7 ♢ A Q 10 ♣ A J 6 5 4

8. ♠ K Q 9 ♡ A Q ♢ J 4 ♣ A J 9 8 4 3

9. ♠ 5 ♡ 8 7 3 ♢ A 6 4 ♣ A K Q 10 9 2

10. ♠ K Q ♡ K J ♢ A K ♣ Q 8 7 6 4 3 2

11. ♠ 10 ♡ K 7 5 ♢ A 6 3 2 ♣ A K J 5 3

12. ♠ A Q J ♡ 8 ♢ K Q 7 2 ♣ A K 6 5 3

13. ♠ — ♡ A 7 4 ♢ A J 10 8 ♣ A K 8 7 4 2

14. ♠ K J 8 ♡ A 4 ♢ 6 ♣ A K Q 8 7 6 4

Opener Rebids after 1♣ – 1♢

1. ♠ K Q 9 ♡ A J 7 5 ♢ Q ♣ A Q 6 5 3

Bid 1♡. You are definitely not strong enough for a 2♡ jump-shift, which is game-forcing *no matter what partner has*. You can't make game opposite 6 HCP, but also keep in mind that responder might have only 5 HCP, or even 4 HCP with a singleton club — in which case he bid 1♢ because he was unwilling to watch you struggle in 1♣.

Your 1♡ bid is not forcing, but if responder passes, you will have no regrets about staying low. Because opener's jump-shift starts at 19, **his non-jump new suit can be as strong as 18 HCP.** Therefore, if responder has 8 or more HCP, he should not pass opener's 1-level rebid in a suit. When nothing appeals to responder, he can temporize by bidding 1NT.

2. ♠ A K Q J ♡ 5 4 3 2 ♢ — ♣ Q J 9 8 4

Bid 1♠. Conventional wisdom dictates an up the line 1♡ bid, but with a very attractive alternative (spades), I prefer to not introduce the puny hearts. Although "length is more important than strength," the strength of your suits *does* matter.

3. ♠ Q 7 5 2 ♡ K J 3 ♢ A 9 8 ♣ Q J 4

Bid 1NT. **After you open 1♣ with a totally flat hand, NEVER introduce a 4-card major at your second turn. Instead, bid notrump ASAP.** With this distribution, there's no advantage in trying to play in a suit contract. This concept is similar to the idea of responder ignoring his major suit with 4-3-3-3 after partner opens 1NT.

4.   ♠ Q 2   ♡ 8 7 4 3   ◇ A   ♣ K Q J 10 8 6
Bid 2♣. This bid describes your minimum hand and great suit very nicely. Ignoring this pathetic major shouldn't bother you at all.

5.   ♠ 5 2   ♡ K 7 3   ◇ A K J   ♣ Q 8 7 5 2
Bid 2◇. You would like to avoid a notrump rebid with a worthless doubleton in an unbid suit. You have three honors in partner's suit, so let him know how fond you are of diamonds.

6.   ♠ 4   ♡ A K J   ◇ J 4 3   ♣ A K Q J 10 3
Bid 2♡. No one likes introducing a major suit with three cards, but you are much too strong for an invitational jump to 3♣. Your jump-shift is game-forcing, and will make it easy for your side to explore for the best contract. If partner raises hearts, you'll rebid 4♣ and hope for the best.

7.   ♠ A K 8 6   ♡ 7   ◇ A Q 10   ♣ A J 6 5 4
Bid 2♠. Despite having only 18 HCP, this hand is loaded with upgrades. You have three aces, a useful holding in partner's suit, and a singleton. If partner had responded in hearts, you would have feared a misfit and settled for 1♠.

8.   ♠ K Q 9   ♡ A Q   ◇ J 4   ♣ A J 9 8 4 3
Bid 2NT. The potential of your 6-card suit allows you to jump in notrump, despite having only 17 HCP. With such good stoppers in the majors, 2NT is more helpful to partner than jumping in clubs. You are ready, willing, and able to invite 3NT.

Opener Rebids after 1♣ – 1◇

9. ♠ 5 ♡ 8 7 3 ◇ A 6 4 ♣ A K Q 10 9 2
Bid 3♣. With a *great* suit, opener doesn't need a lot of HCP for the invitational jump in his suit.

10. ♠ K Q ♡ K J ◇ A K ♣ Q 8 7 6 4 3 2
Bid 3♣. With a *weak* suit, opener can make the same bid with as many as 18 HCP.

11. ♠ 10 ♡ K 7 5 ◇ A 6 3 2 ♣ A K J 5 3
Bid 3◇. Your jump raise invites game. Of course, if responder has a big hand, the sky's the limit.

12. ♠ A Q J ♡ 8 ◇ K Q 7 2 ♣ A K 6 5 3
Bid 3♡. This alertable, artificial splinter bid promises a game-forcing raise of partner's suit as well as a singleton or void in hearts. If your partnership doesn't play splinter bids, your correct bid would be an imperfect jump to 2♠.

13. ♠ — ♡ A 7 4 ◇ A J 10 8 ♣ A K 8 7 4 2
Bid 3♠. With a fit and a void, your hand is now HUGE. You have first-round control of all four suits, which does not happen every day. Partner needs next-to-nothing to produce a game or slam.

14. ♠ K J 8 ♡ A 4 ◇ 6 ♣ A K Q 8 7 6 4
Bid 3NT. **Opener's double jump to 3NT always shows an unbalanced hand with length and strength in the suit you opened.** With a strong (18-19 HCP) balanced hand, you would jump to 2NT, and with 20-21, you'd open 2NT.

Avoiding a 4-4 "Fit"

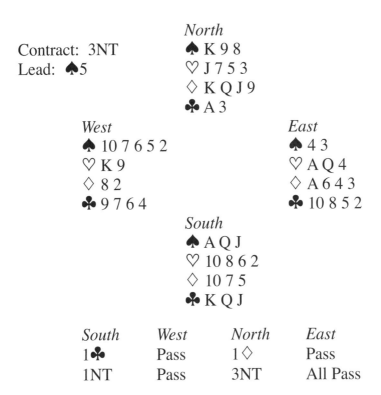

Contract: 3NT
Lead: ♠5

North
♠ K 9 8
♡ J 7 5 3
◇ K Q J 9
♣ A 3

West
♠ 10 7 6 5 2
♡ K 9
◇ 8 2
♣ 9 7 6 4

East
♠ 4 3
♡ A Q 4
◇ A 6 4 3
♣ 10 8 5 2

South
♠ A Q J
♡ 10 8 6 2
◇ 10 7 5
♣ K Q J

South	West	North	East
1♣	Pass	1◇	Pass
1NT	Pass	3NT	All Pass

The outcome in 3NT was never in doubt. Declarer knocked out the ◇A and won three diamond tricks, three clubs and three spades. If North-South had reached 4♡, the result would have been equally obvious. South would lose three hearts and the ◇A, and finish down one.

The key to the happy ending was South's decision to suppress her 4-card major and rebid 1NT. With 4-3-3-3 distribution, there is no advantage to playing in a suit, so South correctly bid notrump at her second turn. In addition, the 1NT rebid gives responder an immediate description of opener's minimum, balanced hand.

19

Chapter 2

Opener Rebids after 1♣ – 1♡

For each of these hands, what should opener bid now?

1. ♠ A 10 9 7 ♡ 7 6 ◇ A ♣ K Q J 9 5 4

2. ♠ 6 5 4 2 ♡ K J ◇ K Q J ♣ Q J 10 4

3. ♠ 7 5 2 ♡ A K ◇ 8 5 2 ♣ A J 5 4 2

4. ♠ K 9 ♡ K Q ◇ 10 8 5 4 ♣ A 9 6 5 3

5. ♠ Q 9 3 ♡ – ◇ A K Q 10 ♣ A 8 7 5 3 2

6. ♠ 5 2 ♡ K Q ◇ A K J 5 ♣ A K 9 8 7

7. ♠ 7 ♡ A 3 2 ◇ A K Q ♣ A 8 6 5 4 3

8. ♠ 8 ♡ A K 7 ◇ 9 6 4 3 ♣ A J 8 4 2

9. ♠ A Q J 10 4 ♡ 7 ◇ 8 ♣ A K J 9 6 4

10. ♠ A Q ♡ A Q ◇ Q 6 4 3 ♣ K J 6 5 4

11. ♠ A 8 4 ♡ 10 4 ◇ A 3 ♣ K Q J 10 9 3

12. ♠ 9 ♡ A Q 9 7 ◇ 8 6 3 ♣ A K 9 7 6

13. ♠ J 5 3 ♡ K Q J 3 ◇ K Q J ♣ K Q J

14. ♠ 6 ♡ K J 10 5 ◇ A K 9 ♣ K Q J 8 2

15. ♠ A 2 ♡ 3 ◇ 9 7 4 ♣ A K Q J 5 4 3

16. ♠ A 5 ♡ K Q 10 9 ◇ 7 3 ♣ A K 10 5 3

Opener Rebids after 1♣ – 1♡

1. ♠ A 10 9 7 ♡ 7 6 ◇ A ♣ K Q J 9 5 4

Bid 1♠. **Most 6-4 hands should show the 4-card suit before rebidding the 6-bagger.** You can remember this by chanting: "6-4-6," as opposed to "6-6-4."

2. ♠ 6 5 4 2 ♡ K J ◇ K Q J ♣ Q J 10 4

Bid 1NT. Everything about this ugly hand is screaming "notrump." You have soft cards and terrible spades. It's possible that you'll miss a 4-4 spade fit, but, even if you have one, there is no guarantee that a spade contract will be worthwhile with *this* hand. The 1NT rebid both describes and limits your hand, while a 1♠ rebid is ambiguous about your strength and distribution.

3. ♠ 7 5 2 ♡ A K ◇ 8 5 2 ♣ A J 5 4 2

Bid 1NT. With no semblance of a stopper in either unbid suit, this is hardly appetizing; but your only alternative is to bid 2♣. Yuck! **Opener should not rebid a 5-card suit after a 1-level response in a suit.**

4. ♠ K 9 ♡ K Q ◇ 10 8 5 4 ♣ A 9 6 5 3

Bid 1NT. You can't be concerned about having two doubletons. Once you sensibly decided to open 1♣, you were committed to rebidding 1NT after partner's major-suit response.

5. ♠ Q 9 3 ♡ — ◇ A K Q 10 ♣ A 8 7 5 3 2

Bid 2♣. Yes, your diamonds are exquisite, but a 2◇ reverse is out of the question. You have a misfit for partner's hearts, a weak long suit, a dubious ♠Q, and *only* 15 HCP.

6.   ♠ 5 2   ♡ K Q   ◇ A K J 5   ♣ A K 9 8 7

Bid 2◇. A perfect hand for a reverse, which is forcing for one round. With your 20 HCP, you plan to force to game. You might not love reverse auctions, but it is nice to have an economical, forcing bid available.

7.   ♠ 7   ♡ A 3 2   ◇ A K Q   ♣ A 8 6 5 4 3

Bid 2◇. A reverse into a 3-card suit is *not* ideal, but your alternatives are less attractive. Not only are your clubs too weak to jump to 3♣, but such a non-economical bid would crowd the auction and make it difficult to find a possible 5-3 heart fit. **Marty Sez: With a choice of imperfect bids, the cheaper the better.**

8.   ♠ 8   ♡ A K 7   ◇ 9 6 4 3   ♣ A J 8 4 2

Bid 2♡. You have a ruffing value and three trumps headed by the two top honors, so you should be delighted to raise.

9.   ♠ A Q J 10 4   ♡ 7   ◇ 8   ♣ A K J 9 6 4

Bid 2♠. With a 6-5 hand that includes two lovely suits, you don't need a lot of HCP to force to game. When you rebid spades at your next turn, you will be promising five spades and six clubs; because you would have opened 1♠ with 5-5.

10.   ♠ A Q   ♡ A Q   ◇ Q 6 4 3   ♣ K J 6 5 4

Bid 2NT. Why prefer the offshape 2NT to a 2◇ reverse? The jump to 2NT shows 18-19 HCP and invites game, but can be passed. A reverse promises 17 HCP *or more;* you might be inviting game, but might have a game-forcing hand. **Don't be vague when you can be precise.**

Opener Rebids after 1♣ – 1♡

11. ♠ A 8 4 ♡ 10 4 ◇ A 3 ♣ K Q J 10 9 3
Bid 3♣. With seven sure tricks, a 2♣ rebid would be
a serious underbid.

12. ♠ 9 ♡ A Q 9 7 ◇ 8 6 3 ♣ A K 9 7 6
Bid 3♡, not 2♡. After the 1♡ response, this is NOT a
minimum opening bid. 3½ quick tricks is the maximum
possible for a hand with 13 HCP, and you love the fact that
your honors are concentrated in your two longest suits.

13. ♠ J 5 3 ♡ K Q J 3 ◇ K Q J ♣ K Q J
Bid 3♡, not 4♡. Despite your 19 HCP, a raise to three
is plenty with this aceless, 4-3-3-3, six-loser hand.

14. ♠ 6 ♡ K J 10 5 ◇ A K 9 ♣ K Q J 8 2
Bid 3♠. This splinter raise shows a hand strong enough
to raise to 4♡ **AND** a singleton or void in spades.

15. ♠ A 2 ♡ 3 ◇ 9 7 4 ♣ A K Q J 5 4 3
Bid 3NT, not 3♣. Because you need so little help from
partner to make this, don't worry about diamonds.

16. ♠ A 5 ♡ K Q 10 9 ◇ 7 3 ♣ A K 10 5 3
Bid 4♡. Tell the truth: if you made the textbook bid of
3♡, wouldn't you feel terrible if responder declined your
invitation? Despite having no singleton and "only" 16
HCP, this is a very upgradable hand. Why? Four quick
tricks, three trump honors, and a source of tricks in clubs.

Stopping on a Dime

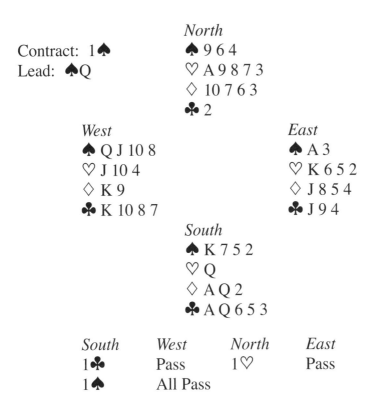

Contract: 1♠
Lead: ♠Q

North
♠ 9 6 4
♡ A 9 8 7 3
♢ 10 7 6 3
♣ 2

West
♠ Q J 10 8
♡ J 10 4
♢ K 9
♣ K 10 8 7

East
♠ A 3
♡ K 6 5 2
♢ J 8 5 4
♣ J 9 4

South
♠ K 7 5 2
♡ Q
♢ A Q 2
♣ A Q 6 5 3

South	West	North	East
1♣	Pass	1♡	Pass
1♠	All Pass		

South had 17 HCP, but contented herself with a 1♠ rebid. She was disappointed when North passed, but with North's sub-minimum hand, even seven tricks were not guaranteed.

East won the trump lead with his ♠A, and fired back a trump to South's ♠K. Declarer needed three ruffs to go along with her four top tricks. Before ruffing a club with dummy's last trump, she set her sights on *two* heart ruffs.

South led the ♡Q to the ace, and ruffed a heart. She cashed the ♣A and ruffed a club. She scored her sixth trick by ruffing another heart with her last trump, and the ♢A furnished trick #7.

Chapter 3

Opener Rebids after 1♢ – 1♡

For each of these hands, what should opener bid now?

1.   ♠ 10 9 7 3   ♡ A 7   ♢ A K Q 9   ♣ 8 5 4

2.   ♠ 10 9 7 3   ♡ A K Q   ♢ A Q 8 6 5   ♣ J

3.   ♠ 10 9 7 3   ♡ A K Q   ♢ A 8 6 5   ♣ 5 4

4.   ♠ A Q   ♡ A K   ♢ 9 8 6 3 2   ♣ 9 6 5 3

5.   ♠ Q 7   ♡ J 5 3   ♢ K Q 10 9   ♣ K Q 8 2

6.   ♠ 8 4   ♡ 5   ♢ A K 8 7 5 3   ♣ A K J 3

7.   ♠ 8 4   ♡ 5   ♢ A K J 10 9 5   ♣ K 7 5 3

8.   ♠ K Q   ♡ K 7 5 2   ♢ J 6 5 3   ♣ K 6 4

9.   ♠ A 6 4   ♡ A 10 9 8   ♢ A Q 10 9   ♣ 6 3

10.   ♠ A K 9 5   ♡ A 10 8   ♢ A K J 9   ♣ 4 2

11.   ♠ K J   ♡ Q 9   ♢ A Q 10 6 4   ♣ A Q 7 6

12.   ♠ 8   ♡ 7 6   ♢ A K Q J 8 5   ♣ A K 9 6

13.   ♠ Q   ♡ A Q   ♢ K Q J 9 8 3   ♣ K 5 3 2

14.   ♠ K J   ♡ A Q 5 3   ♢ Q 8 6 5 3 2   ♣ A

Opener Rebids after 1◇ – 1♡

1. ♠ 10 9 7 3   ♡ A 7   ◇ A K Q 9   ♣ 8 5 4
Bid 1♠. After 1◇ – 1♡, opener should be eager to
show his 4-card spade suit, even if the suit lacks quality.
Because of the up the line principle, responder may also
have four spades when he responds 1♡.

2. ♠ 10 9 7 3   ♡ A K Q   ◇ A Q 8 6 5   ♣ J
Bid 1♠. If responder bids 1NT or 2◇ at his second turn,
you'll bid 2♡. This sequence of bids promises more than
a minimum hand with four spades, three hearts, 5-6
diamonds and 0-1 club. Very descriptive.

3. ♠ 10 9 7 3   ♡ A K Q   ◇ A 8 6 5   ♣ 5 4
Bid 2♡, not 1♠. This hand is a logical exception. Instead
of showing your 4-card spade suit, you should describe
your hand in one bid by raising to 2♡. This hand is not
strong enough to bid spades now and hearts later.

4. ♠ A Q   ♡ A K   ◇ 9 8 6 3 2   ♣ 9 6 5 3
Bid 1NT. The normal rebid with this distribution is 2♣,
but with your weak minors and strong majors, 1NT is more
descriptive.

5. ♠ Q 7   ♡ J 5 3   ◇ K Q 10 9   ♣ K Q 8 2
Bid 1NT. Some players would rebid 2♣, but opener
should not show both minors with a balanced hand.
NEVER open 1◇ and rebid 2♣ after a 1♡ response
with less than nine cards in the minors. **Opener's 1NT
rebid does not promise stoppers in the unbid suits.**

6. ♠ 8 4   ♡ 5   ♢ A K 8 7 5 3   ♣ A K J 3

Bid 2♣, rather than 3♢. These clubs are too good to ignore. If the bidding continues, you'll still have a chance to let partner know that you have six diamonds.

7. ♠ 8 4   ♡ 5   ♢ A K J 10 9 5   ♣ K 7 5 3

Bid 2♢. With fabulous diamonds, mediocre clubs, and a minimum hand, 2♢ is a standout.

8. ♠ K Q   ♡ K 7 5 2   ♢ J 6 5 3   ♣ K 6 4

Bid 2♡. Some players (myself included) would not have opened this aceless, spotless collection.

9. ♠ A 6 4   ♡ A 10 9 8   ♢ A Q 10 9   ♣ 6 3

What's the problem, you ask? Isn't this a routine raise to 2♡ with your balanced 14-count? Not so fast. This hand is loaded with upgrades.

I'm sure you'll agree that this hand is a lot better than hand #8. This one has 3½ quick tricks, while the previous hand has only two. In addition, I hope that you appreciated all of your intermediates — they will often result in extra tricks. These upgrades make this hand worth a jump to 3♡.

Because of all the upgrades, I recommend opening the last hand 1NT. And if partner transfers to hearts, I would be delighted to jump to 3♡ with this maximum in support of hearts. Points, schmoints!

Opener Rebids after 1♢ – 1♡

10.   ♠ A K 9 5   ♡ A 10 8   ♢ A K J 9   ♣ 4 2

Bid 2♠. Opener's jump-shift is usually based on an unbalanced hand. However, with an upgradable 19-count that includes five quick tricks and a potential heart fit, you should be willing to force to game. If you had "added a point" for the quick tricks and intermediates and opened 2NT, I agree 100%.

11.   ♠ K J   ♡ Q 9   ♢ A Q 10 6 4   ♣ A Q 7 6

Bid 2NT. A sensible compromise between a game-forcing 3♣ (overbid), and a wide-range 2♣ (11-18 HCP).

12.   ♠ 8   ♡ 7 6   ♢ A K Q J 8 5   ♣ A K 9 6

Bid 3♣. You love having all your honors in your long suits. If partner has a spade stopper, you expect to make 3NT even if he has a terrible hand. **Hands with solid suits should always be upgraded.**

13.   ♠ Q   ♡ A Q   ♢ K Q J 9 8 3   ♣ K 5 3 2

Bid 3♢. Same distribution and 17 HCP as hand #12, but forcing to game is out of the question. With lovely diamonds and weak clubs, you prefer rebidding your nice 6-bagger rather than showing your indifferent 4-card suit.

14.   ♠ K J   ♡ A Q 5 3   ♢ Q 8 6 5 3 2   ♣ A

Bid 3♡. You are clearly too good for a single raise, but with half your strength in your short suits, this hand is only worth an invitation. Unless responder has diamond help, the value of your long suit is questionable.

The ♡6 Saves the Day in 3NT

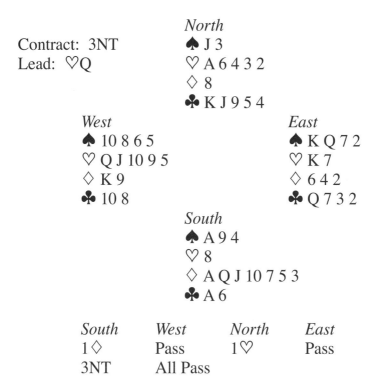

Contract: 3NT
Lead: ♡Q

North
♠ J 3
♡ A 6 4 3 2
◇ 8
♣ K J 9 5 4

West
♠ 10 8 6 5
♡ Q J 10 9 5
◇ K 9
♣ 10 8

East
♠ K Q 7 2
♡ K 7
◇ 6 4 2
♣ Q 7 3 2

South
♠ A 9 4
♡ 8
◇ A Q J 10 7 5 3
♣ A 6

South	West	North	East
1◇	Pass	1♡	Pass
3NT	All Pass		

Once North responded in hearts, South was ready to insist on game with her 8½ playing tricks, and wasted no time jumping to the 9-trick game.

The heart lead threatened declarer, but because she feared a spade switch, she won the first trick. East was on his toes, and unblocked his king. However, when West won his ◇K and began running hearts, North's ♡6 limited the defense to three heart tricks and one diamond.

A spade lead would not have defeated the contract. South would have won the ♠A and played diamonds, and only lost three spades and one diamond. The only lead to defeat the contract was the ♡5!

31

Chapter 4

Opener Rebids after 1♣ − 1♠

For each of these hands, what should opener bid now?

1.   ♠ 4   ♡ A K J 9   ◇ J 9 4   ♣ K 10 4 3 2

2.   ♠ A K   ♡ K J 5 2   ◇ 3 2   ♣ Q 8 6 5 3

3.   ♠ K Q   ♡ 3 2   ◇ 7 5 4 2   ♣ A Q J 10 9

4.   ♠ K 10 8   ♡ −   ◇ A K 5 4   ♣ A 10 9 6 4 3

5.   ♠ J   ♡ A K Q J   ◇ J 2   ♣ K 7 6 5 4 2

6.   ♠ 8 7   ♡ A 10 9 3   ◇ A Q 7   ♣ A K 10 8

7.   ♠ K   ♡ 8 7 5 4   ◇ A K Q   ♣ A Q 7 6 2

8.   ♠ K Q J 5   ♡ K J 9   ◇ K J 9   ♣ K J 7

9.   ♠ Q 7   ♡ 8   ◇ 7 5   ♣ A K Q J 10 5 3 2

10.   ♠ A 7 6 4   ♡ K Q   ◇ K J   ♣ K J 9 5 4

11.   ♠ A J 10 9   ♡ 6 4   ◇ A 6   ♣ A K 9 8 5

12.   ♠ A 6   ♡ A Q   ◇ K 10   ♣ A J 9 5 4 3 2

13.   ♠ K Q 8 7   ♡ A   ◇ A Q 3   ♣ K 8 7 6 4

14.   ♠ A 10 7 3   ♡ A 9 8   ◇ A 4   ♣ A K 6 4

Opener Rebids after 1♣ – 1♠

1. ♠ 4 ♡ A K J 9 ◇ J 9 4 ♣ K 10 4 3 2

Bid 1NT, not 2♣. After a 1♠ response, opener will often have no alternative to rebidding 1NT with a minimum hand and a singleton spade. Players who choose to open 4-card majors avoid the problem by opening 1♡ with this distribution whenever their minimum opening bid includes strong hearts.

2. ♠ A K ♡ K J 5 2 ◇ 3 2 ♣ Q 8 6 5 3

Bid 1NT. Because a 2♡ reverse would promise a very strong hand (usually 17 HCP), that's not an option here. Therefore, you should rebid 1NT, despite a worthless doubleton in an unbid suit.

3. ♠ K Q ♡ 3 2 ◇ 7 5 4 2 ♣ A Q J 10 9

Bid 2♣. A rare example of correctly rebidding a 5-card suit after a 1-level response in a suit. If your 2♣ bid ends the auction, you are guaranteed to win at least four trump tricks even if partner lacks support. **Any suit containing four honors can be treated as if it were one card longer.**

4. ♠ K 10 8 ♡ — ◇ A K 5 4 ♣ A 10 9 6 4 3

Bid 2◇. You planned to rebid 2♣ after the expected 1♡ response, but, after partner responded in your longer major, things are looking up.

It's true that raising to 2♠ is a better option than rebidding 2♣, but with a *useful* void and 3½ quick tricks, you're too strong for a single raise. **With a very upgradable opening bid, you can reverse with less than 17 HCP.**

5.　　♠ J　♡ A K Q J　◇ J 2　♣ K 7 6 5 4 2

Bid 2♣, not 2♡. We love 6-4 hands and suits with 100 honors, but a reverse is out of the question. Your clubs are weak, and your honors in spades and diamonds are questionable.

6.　　♠ 8 7　♡ A 10 9 3　◇ A Q 7　♣ A K 10 8

Bid 2NT. Because of the three aces and nice spot cards, you correctly evaluated this hand as too strong for a 1NT opening bid. Describing this hand as a balanced 18-count is definitely not an overstatement.

7.　　♠ K　♡ 8 7 5 4　◇ A K Q　♣ A Q 7 6 2

Bid a practical 2NT, as opposed to a 2♡ reverse. You try to avoid jumping to 2NT with a singleton, but it does give a good overall description of *this* hand. There is no question that notrump auctions are preferable to reverse auctions. In addition, you aren't really eager to talk about your mangy hearts.

8.　　♠ K Q J 5　♡ K J 9　◇ K J 9　♣ K J 7

Bid 2NT! No, this is not a misprint. You do have great spade support, but your tenaces and lack of shape are screaming for you to become declarer in notrump.

You could have avoided this "non-support" fib. Despite your 18 HCP, you should have opened 1NT. You have: 4-3-3-3 distribution, with too many jacks, no aces, and only 2½ quick tricks. If ever a hand demanded downgrading, this is it.

Opener Rebids after 1♣ – 1♠

9.　♠ Q 7　♡ 8　♢ 7 5　♣ A K Q J 10 5 3 2

Bid 3♣. With eight tricks, you're too strong to rebid 2♣.
If you play "Gambling 3NT," you would open this hand
3NT; promising a solid minor with no outside ace or king.
This convention gives a very good description of this hand,
and allows responder to decide whether or not to play 3NT.

10.　♠ A 7 6 4　♡ K Q　♢ K J　♣ K J 9 5 4

Bid 3♠, not 4♠. Your red-suit honors are not pulling their
full weight. Tread lightly with hands that contain too many
honors in short suits. If partner passes 3♠, you will have
no regrets.

11.　♠ A J 10 9　♡ 6 4　♢ A 6　♣ A K 9 8 5

Bid 4♠, not 3♠. Same shape and fewer HCP than hand
#10; but you love your trump intermediates and four quick
tricks, and are unwilling to risk stopping in 3♠.

12.　♠ A 6　♡ A Q　♢ K 10　♣ A J 9 5 4 3 2

Bid 3NT. You would be happier if your long suit were
stronger, but it *is* a 7-card suit with two honors. No other
rebid comes close to expressing the potential of this hand.

13.　♠ K Q 8 7　♡ A　♢ A Q 3　♣ K 8 7 6 4

Bid 4♡. Because of the singleton ace, this is an imperfect
splinter bid. Nevertheless, it is the most descriptive bid.

14.　♠ A 10 7 3　♡ A 9 8　♢ A 4　♣ A K 6 4

Bid 4♠, inviting slam. Note: I don't agree with the 1♣
opening bid. With four aces and five quick tricks, you
should have added a point (or two) and opened 2NT.

A Sensible 3-Card Raise

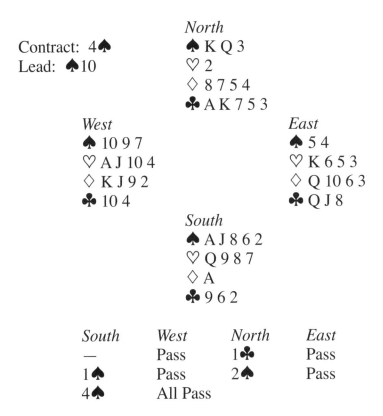

Contract: 4♠
Lead: ♠10

North
♠ K Q 3
♥ 2
♦ 8 7 5 4
♣ A K 7 5 3

West
♠ 10 9 7
♥ A J 10 4
♦ K J 9 2
♣ 10 4

East
♠ 5 4
♥ K 6 5 3
♦ Q 10 6 3
♣ Q J 8

South
♠ A J 8 6 2
♥ Q 9 8 7
♦ A
♣ 9 6 2

South	West	North	East
—	Pass	1♣	Pass
1♠	Pass	2♠	Pass
4♠	All Pass		

North was delighted to raise spades with his excellent 3-card support, and South was happy to jump to game.

Declarer needed to set up dummy's club suit, but had to keep a trump in dummy to ensure that the defense could not take too many heart tricks.

South won the opening lead with the ♠K and ducked a club. Because of dummy's trumps, the defense was unable to run hearts. Declarer won East's diamond shift, and led a club to the ♣A. She then drew trumps and ran clubs. South won 10 tricks: four clubs, five spades, and the ◇A.

Chapter 5

Opener Rebids after 1◇ – 1♠

For each of these hands, what should opener bid now?

1. ♠ J 8 7 ♡ A 7 ◇ A 8 6 4 2 ♣ A 5 3

2. ♠ J 8 7 ♡ A Q ◇ Q 8 6 4 2 ♣ K J 9

3. ♠ Q J 6 ♡ K J 7 ◇ Q J 7 3 ♣ K Q 7

4. ♠ A 10 ♡ Q 8 ◇ K 10 8 7 ♣ A 8 7 4 2

5. ♠ K J 8 ♡ 2 ◇ K Q 7 5 3 ♣ K 6 4 3

6. ♠ 10 8 3 ♡ J ◇ A K J 5 3 ♣ A K 4 2

7. ♠ A K ♡ A K J ◇ 9 7 6 5 3 2 ♣ 8 4

8. ♠ K Q 7 ♡ A K 5 ◇ A Q J 9 8 3 ♣ 2

9. ♠ 8 6 4 3 ♡ K Q J ◇ K Q J 5 3 ♣ K

10. ♠ A J 5 ♡ 7 5 ◇ K Q J 10 9 5 ♣ 8 2

11. ♠ K J 10 ♡ A 5 3 ◇ A 7 6 5 4 2 ♣ 7

12. ♠ A J 2 ♡ 9 7 6 ◇ A K Q 5 ♣ A 7 2

13. ♠ K 7 3 ♡ 3 ◇ A K Q 9 5 4 2 ♣ A Q

14. ♠ 8 4 ♡ A K ◇ A Q 10 9 7 5 3 ♣ 8 6

15. ♠ A K J ♡ 7 2 ◇ A 8 6 5 3 2 ♣ A 4

16. ♠ 8 7 4 2 ♡ A ◇ A K Q J 7 5 ♣ K Q

17. ♠ K Q 8 7 ♡ A Q ◇ A J 10 6 4 ♣ K J

Opener Rebids after 1◇ – 1♠

1.   ♠ J 8 7   ♡ A 7   ◇ A 8 6 4 2   ♣ A 5 3
Bid 2♠, not 1NT. Hands with "aces and spaces" play better in a suit contract than in notrump.

2.   ♠ J 8 7   ♡ A Q   ◇ Q 8 6 4 2   ♣ K J 9
Bid 1NT, not 2♠. The identical distribution, 13 HCP, and spade holding as in the previous hand, but the scattered honors suggest notrump. You'd like to become declarer in order to protect your tenaces in hearts and clubs.

3.   ♠ Q J 6   ♡ K J 7   ◇ Q J 7 3   ♣ K Q 7
Bid 1NT. Despite your 15 HCP, I hope that you wouldn't open 1NT with this trash. The trick-taking potential of this hand is extremely limited.

4.   ♠ A 10   ♡ Q 8   ◇ K 10 8 7   ♣ A 8 7 4 2
Bid 2♣. This is clear; the only question was what to open. If the diamonds were *any* weaker, I'd open 1♣, and then rebid 1NT after a 1♡ or 1♠ response.

5.   ♠ K J 8   ♡ 2   ◇ K Q 7 5 3   ♣ K 6 4 3
Bid 2♠, not 2♣. The raise is more helpful to partner than showing your other minor. **With a minimum opening bid, you must not be afraid to raise responder's major with 3-card support.**

6.   ♠ 10 8 3   ♡ J   ◇ A K J 5 3   ♣ A K 4 2
Bid 2♣. You're too strong to raise to 2♠, but not strong enough for any jump. If partner doesn't pass, you'll show your 3-card spade support next, allowing partner to select the best contract.

7.   ♠ A K ♡ A K J ◊ 9 7 6 5 3 2 ♣ 8 4

Bid 2◊. You usually don't have as many as 15 HCP for this minimum rebid, and rebidding a nine-high suit is not wonderful; but all alternatives are even less appealing *now*. The best way to avoid this scenario is to open 1NT. This may seem unorthodox, but it is the most practical bid.

8.   ♠ K Q 7 ♡ A K 5 ◊ A Q J 9 8 3 ♣ 2

Bid 2♡. A reverse into a 3-card suit is *not* pretty, but there is no second choice. You are far too good for an invitational 3◊ bid, and are not ready to raise spades or bid notrump.

Don't be nervous. Because responder will go up the line with four cards in each major, if partner does raise your hearts, he guarantees five spades — so you'll be delighted to support spades.

9.   ♠ 8 6 4 3 ♡ K Q J ◊ K Q J 5 3 ♣ K

Bid 2♠. I hope you're not tempted to jump. You have terrible trumps, no aces, and a questionable club honor.

10.   ♠ A J 5 ♡ 7 5 ◊ K Q J 10 9 5 ♣ 8 2

Bid 2◊, not 2♠. You could support spades, but if partner is not worth a second bid, you'd prefer that diamonds become the trump suit.

11.   ♠ K J 10 ♡ A 5 3 ◊ A 7 6 5 4 2 ♣ 7

Bid 2♠. Many players would rebid their 6-card suit, but your three spade honors are impressive, while *these* diamonds are not worth showing off.

12. ♠ A J 2 ♡ 9 7 6 ◇ A K Q 5 ♣ A 7 2
Bid 2NT. You are concerned about the unbid major, but 2NT does describe your balanced 18-count perfectly. Any other bid would be a distortion.

13. ♠ K 7 3 ♡ 3 ◇ A K Q 9 5 4 2 ♣ A Q
Bid 3♣. What else can you do? A non-forcing 3◇ would be a gross underbid. You planned to jump to 3NT after a 1♡ response, but you can hardly bid 3NT with a small singleton in an *unbid* major. Don't worry; if partner raises clubs, you'll overrule him in diamonds. **When you must tell a lie, it is better to do so in a lower-ranking suit.**

14. ♠ 8 4 ♡ A K ◇ A Q 10 9 7 5 3 ♣ 8 6
Bid 3◇. With an excellent 7-card suit, opener can make the invitational jump in his suit without a lot of HCP.

15. ♠ A K J ♡ 7 2 ◇ A 8 6 5 3 2 ♣ A 4
Bid 3♠. A VERY rare case of opener's jump raise with only 3-card support. This is not ideal, but your spades are very attractive, while your alternatives are not.

16. ♠ 8 7 4 2 ♡ A ◇ A K Q J 7 5 ♣ K Q
Bid 4♡. If responder signs off in 4♠, you should bite the bullet and pass. Although this hand has great potential, it's not as good as it looks because of the weak spades.

17. ♠ K Q 8 7 ♡ A Q ◇ A J 10 6 4 ♣ K J
Bid 4♠. This hand should have been opened 2NT, despite the two doubletons. Your tenaces in the rounded suits (hearts and clubs) were shouting, "grab the notrump!"

Opener's Jump-Shift

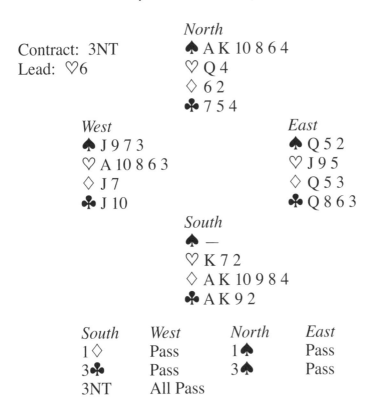

Contract: 3NT
Lead: ♡6

North
♠ A K 10 8 6 4
♡ Q 4
♢ 6 2
♣ 7 5 4

West
♠ J 9 7 3
♡ A 10 8 6 3
♢ J 7
♣ J 10

East
♠ Q 5 2
♡ J 9 5
♢ Q 5 3
♣ Q 8 6 3

South
♠ —
♡ K 7 2
♢ A K 10 9 8 4
♣ A K 9 2

South	West	North	East
1♢	Pass	1♠	Pass
3♣	Pass	3♠	Pass
3NT	All Pass		

Despite the void in partner's suit, South liked her 4½ quick tricks and long, strong suit, and forced to game.

Declarer was careful to put up dummy's ♡Q at trick one. When this won, her ♡K7 provided protection from any future heart attack *as long as East did not obtain the lead.*

South needed to develop diamonds, and was willing to lose a trick to West. At trick two, she cashed the ♠A, and discarded the ♣2. Then she led a diamond to her ♢10. West won the jack, but was helpless. He exited with the ♣J, but South won the ♣A and ran diamonds. The ♣K was her ninth trick.

Chapter 6

Opener Rebids after 1♡ – 1♠

For each of these hands, what should opener bid now?

1.   ♠ A Q   ♡ A Q 8 7 2   ♢ 7 5 4   ♣ 7 5 4

2.   ♠ A Q   ♡ J 6 5 4 3   ♢ A Q   ♣ 6 5 4 2

3.   ♠ A Q   ♡ A K 10 9 5   ♢ 5 3   ♣ 6 5 4 2

4.   ♠ 9   ♡ A J 9 7 6 3   ♢ K 3   ♣ A Q J 9

5.   ♠ 7   ♡ K Q 10 9 7 5   ♢ A 8   ♣ Q 7 4 3

6.   ♠ 7   ♡ K J 7 5 3   ♢ A Q 10 8 3 2   ♣ 3

7.   ♠ A J   ♡ K J 6 4 2   ♢ A K 5   ♣ 5 4 2

8.   ♠ K Q   ♡ K J 6 5 3 2   ♢ Q J 4   ♣ K J

9.   ♠ A J 9   ♡ A 8 6 4 3   ♢ 8 4   ♣ A 7 3

10.   ♠ K 5 2   ♡ A K J 7 6   ♢ A K   ♣ 8 5 4

11.   ♠ K 9 4   ♡ A Q 7 6 4 3   ♢ A   ♣ K Q J

12.   ♠ Q J 6   ♡ A K J 10 9 5 2   ♢ —   ♣ 7 6 4

13.   ♠ A J 10 7   ♡ A K 9 8 6   ♢ 8 6 5 3   ♣ —

14.   ♠ 8 7   ♡ A K Q J 8 6 3   ♢ K J   ♣ K Q

15.   ♠ A K 10 8   ♡ A K Q 9 6   ♢ 8   ♣ J 5 2

16.   ♠ A 4   ♡ A Q J 9 7 5 4 2   ♢ Q 9 6   ♣ —

Opener Rebids after 1♡ – 1♠

1. ♠ A Q ♡ A Q 8 7 2 ◇ 7 5 4 ♣ 7 5 4

Bid 1NT. Stoppers, schmoppers! When you have a minimum opening bid with this distribution, what else can you do?

2. ♠ A Q ♡ J 6 5 4 3 ◇ A Q ♣ 6 5 4 2

Bid 1NT, not 2♣. Most 2-5-2-4 hands should bid 2♣ on this auction, but 1NT seems more appropriate here, based on your strong diamonds and terrible clubs. With these weak hearts, the last thing you want is for partner to take you back to 2♡ with a doubleton heart. This could easily happen if you bid 2♣ and responder holds a weak hand with two hearts and fewer than six spades or four clubs.

3. ♠ A Q ♡ A K 10 9 5 ◇ 5 3 ♣ 6 5 4 2

Bid 2♣, not 1NT. Same distribution, 13 HCP and terrible clubs. However, with two small diamonds, you would prefer to avoid notrump. In addition, if partner wants to take a preference to hearts, it's okay by you.

4. ♠ 9 ♡ A J 9 7 6 3 ◇ K 3 ♣ A Q J 9

Bid 2♣, not 2♡ or 3♡. The hand is strong enough to jump to 3♡, but with 6-4 distribution and a non-minimum hand, it's more flexible to show your impressive second suit while it is easy to do so.

5. ♠ 7 ♡ K Q 10 9 7 5 ◇ A 8 ♣ Q 7 4 3

Bid 2♡, not 2♣. Your hearts are impressive (playable opposite a small singleton), while the clubs are meager and your opening bid is skimpy. Three good reasons to rebid the 6-card suit.

6.　　♠ 7　♡ K J 7 5 3　◇ A Q 10 8 3 2　♣ 3
Bid 2◇. A nice, easy, painless rebid. That is what you had
in mind when you correctly opened 1♡ to facilitate
showing both suits without reversing.

7.　　♠ A J　♡ K J 6 4 2　◇ A K 5　♣ 5 4 2
Bid 2◇. What kind of bridge is this, you ask? "Marty,
I love diamonds as much as anyone, but 3-card suits,
no thank you!"

Have you got any better ideas? You're too strong for 1NT,
but not strong enough to jump to 2NT. There really is no
good alternative at this point.

Of course, you could have avoided this annoying dilemma.
Some players (myself included) would have opened 1NT,
describing this hand completely, except for the 5-card
major. In my experience, I have found that most players
have strong opinions on this subject. The "Hatfields"
open 1♡ and swear by it, while the "McCoys" open 1NT
and are equally adamant. To each his own.

8.　　♠ K Q　♡ K J 6 5 3 2　◇ Q J 4　♣ K J
Bid 2♡, not 3♡. Despite the 16 HCP, your weak suit and
aceless hand suggest taking the low road.

9.　　♠ A J 9　♡ A 8 6 4 3　◇ 8 4　♣ A 7 3
Bid 2♠. With a worthless doubleton in a side suit, you
should prefer raising spades to rebidding 1NT. You have
good 3-card support for spades and three aces, so even if
partner has a weak hand with four spades, your hand will
make a suitable dummy.

Opener Rebids after 1♡ – 1♠

10.　♠K 5 2　♡A K J 7 6　◇A K　♣8 5 4
Bid 2NT. The lack of a club stopper is an imperfection, but any other bid would be a serious distortion.

11.　♠K 9 4　♡A Q 7 6 4 3　◇A　♣K Q J
Bid 3♣. You must force to game, so the "white lie" about your club length is necessary. When opener jump-shifts into a minor, responder should try to avoid raising that suit. With a doubleton heart, he is welcome to bid 3♡.

12.　♠Q J 6　♡A K J 10 9 5 2　◇ —　♣7 6 4
Bid 3♡, not 2♡. Partner's spade response increases the likelihood that your spade honors will be useful.

13.　♠A J 10 7　♡A K 9 8 6　◇8 6 5 3　♣ —
Bid 3♠. Once you find a fit, your club void and three quick tricks justify making a strong rebid.

14.　♠8 7　♡A K Q J 8 6 3　◇K J　♣K Q
Bid 3NT. This alertable double jump shows a terrific hand based on a great heart suit and stoppers in both minors. Partner is welcome to pass, correct to 4♡, or look for slam.

15.　♠A K 10 8　♡A K Q 9 6　◇8　♣J 5 2
Bid 4◇. You would be a lot happier making this splinter bid if you had a club control, but you *are* giving partner a lot of useful information about your hand.

16.　♠A 4　♡A Q J 9 7 5 4 2　◇Q 9 6　♣ —
Bid 4♡. You had too much slam potential to open 4♡. Once partner responds, you must insist on game.

If at First You Don't Succeed....

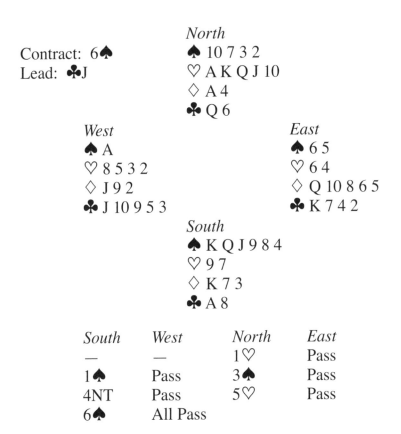

Contract: 6♠
Lead: ♣J

North
♠ 10 7 3 2
♡ A K Q J 10
♢ A 4
♣ Q 6

West
♠ A
♡ 8 5 3 2
♢ J 9 2
♣ J 10 9 5 3

East
♠ 6 5
♡ 6 4
♢ Q 10 8 6 5
♣ K 7 4 2

South
♠ K Q J 9 8 4
♡ 9 7
♢ K 7 3
♣ A 8

South	West	North	East
—	—	1♡	Pass
1♠	Pass	3♠	Pass
4NT	Pass	5♡	Pass
6♠	All Pass		

North's jump to 3♠ invited game. South had a nice hand of her own, and Blackwooded into slam.

West's ♣J lead was covered by the queen, king and ace. Declarer needed to dispose of her club loser on dummy's hearts, and hoped for a 3-3 split. Unfortunately, East ruffed the third round with his ♠5. South overruffed and led her ♢3 to dummy's ace. The fourth heart was also ruffed and overruffed. Declarer cashed the ♢K and ruffed her ♢7. She then led dummy's last heart, discarded her club loser, and conceded the one remaining trump, the ♠A.

Chapter 7

Opener Rebids after 1♣ – 1NT

A 1NT response to 1♣ is unique. A 1NT response to 1♦, 1♡, or 1♠ might include a lower-ranking suit with a hand too weak to respond at the two level. After 1♣, responder can easily show *any* new suit at the one level, so **a 1NT response to 1♣ is always based on a balanced hand.**

Because responder denies a 4-card major, his most likely distribution is 3-3-4-3 (four diamonds).

As for HCP, some partnerships avoid a 1NT response to 1♣ on 6 or even 7 HCP, preferring to respond 1♦ with a weak hand. This is sensible; however, for our purposes, we'll define the 1NT response as 6-10 HCP.

You open 1♣ and partner responds 1NT. Now what?

1. ♠A J 4 ♡Q J 6 ♦K Q J ♣J 7 3 2

2. ♠A 10 7 6 ♡K ♦6 4 3 2 ♣A Q 8 5

3. ♠A ♡K Q 10 5 ♦7 4 2 ♣Q J 9 7 4

4. ♠10 7 5 ♡7 5 4 2 ♦A ♣A K Q 7 2

5. ♠K Q J 9 ♡6 3 ♦K Q ♣J 10 9 8 3

6. ♠J 4 ♡J 5 ♦A K Q 6 ♣A K 8 4 3

7. ♠A 7 ♡K J 4 2 ♦K Q 4 ♣A J 6 3

8. ♠A 7 ♡K J 10 9 ♦K Q 4 ♣A J 10 9

9. ♠A J 3 ♡A 4 ♦9 2 ♣K Q 10 7 6 4

10. ♠A 7 5 3 ♡A K 2 ♦K ♣K Q 10 7 4

11. ♠8 5 3 ♡A ♦K 3 ♣A K 10 8 7 5 2

Opener Rebids after 1♣ – 1NT

1.   ♠ A J 4   ♡ Q J 6   ◇ K Q J   ♣ J 7 3 2
Pass. Despite your 15 HCP, you were correct to
downgrade this junkpile and not open 1NT. You now
have an easy pass. **With a balanced hand not strong
enough to open 1NT, do not raise a 1NT response.**

2.   ♠ A 10 7 6   ♡ K   ◇ 6 4 3 2   ♣ A Q 8 5
Pass. Because partner probably has four diamonds, your
best contract rates to be 2◇. However, if you select that
bid, it would be a forcing reverse. Those players who
always open 1◇ with 4-4 in the minors would be looking
good here; but with such weak diamonds, I totally agree
with the 1♣ opening bid.

3.   ♠ A   ♡ K Q 10 5   ◇ 7 4 2   ♣ Q J 9 7 4
Bid 2♣, instead of passing. Watching partner struggle in
1NT after the expected spade lead wouldn't be much fun.
**Rebidding a 5-card suit with an unbalanced hand is
acceptable when partner guarantees a balanced hand.**

4.   ♠ 10 7 5   ♡ 7 5 4 2   ◇ A   ♣ A K Q 7 2
Pass, instead of bidding 2♣. It's rare to pass 1NT with a
singleton, however.... You expect to deliver six tricks in
clubs or notrump. Regardless of whether you're playing
matchpoints or IMPs, with this hand, seven tricks (in 1NT)
will be easier to make than eight (in 2♣).

5.   ♠ K Q J 9   ♡ 6 3   ◇ K Q   ♣ J 10 9 8 3
Bid 2♣. You have too many aces to knock out —
you won't survive repeated heart attacks in 1NT.

Opener Rebids after 1♣ – 1NT

6.   ♠ J 4   ♡ J 5   ♢ A K Q 6   ♣ A K 8 4 3

Bid 2♢. The reverse is forcing for one round. 3NT is a definite possibility, but unless responder has both majors stopped, your chances aren't good. If partner responds three of a minor, I would call it a day.

7.   ♠ A 7   ♡ K J 4 2   ♢ K Q 4   ♣ A J 6 3

Bid 2NT, not 3NT. If responder has a minimum, this should be high enough.

8.   ♠ A 7   ♡ K J 10 9   ♢ K Q 4   ♣ A J 10 9

Bid 3NT, not 2NT. Check out those lovely intermediates in clubs and hearts. I don't know if you are impressed, but I certainly am.

9.   ♠ A J 3   ♡ A 4   ♢ 9 2   ♣ K Q 10 7 6 4

Bid 3♣, inviting game. If partner has a maximum for his 1NT response, your nice long suit and two aces will give you a great chance to make 3NT.

10.   ♠ A 7 5 3   ♡ A K 2   ♢ K   ♣ K Q 10 7 4

Bid 3NT. Don't be concerned about your singleton ♢K; the opponents will almost certainly lead a major. You've got to be in game, and nine tricks in notrump will be much easier than 11 in clubs.

11.   ♠ 8 5 3   ♡ A   ♢ K 3   ♣ A K 10 8 7 5 2

Bid 3NT. Based on partner's expected three clubs, you should deliver at least seven club tricks and one heart. If you're afraid that partner won't take any tricks, or that the enemy will win the first five, you're worrying too much.

Think Twice Before You Hold Up

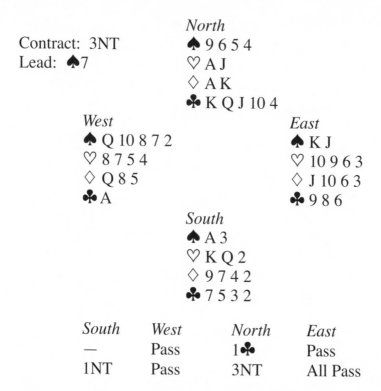

Contract: 3NT
Lead: ♠7

North
♠ 9 6 5 4
♡ A J
◇ A K
♣ K Q J 10 4

West
♠ Q 10 8 7 2
♡ 8 7 5 4
◇ Q 8 5
♣ A

East
♠ K J
♡ 10 9 6 3
◇ J 10 6 3
♣ 9 8 6

South
♠ A 3
♡ K Q 2
◇ 9 7 4 2
♣ 7 5 3 2

South	West	North	East
—	Pass	1♣	Pass
1NT	Pass	3NT	All Pass

South's 1NT response gave a good description of her hand.
North loved his club suit, and jumped to game.

Only a 5-2 spade split would threaten the contract.
If South had held up her ♠A, she would have suffered a
quick defeat when East returned his second spade and
West got in with the ♣A to run spades.

Fortunately, South realized that East had a second spade
honor — West would have led the queen from ♠Q J 10.
If spades were 5-2, the suit had to be blocked. Declarer
won the first trick with her ♠A, and could not be stopped
from scoring up 10 tricks.

Chapter 8

Opener Rebids after 1◇ – 1NT

This 1NT response is somewhat different from 1♣ – 1NT. A 1NT response to a 1◇ opening bid may be based on an unbalanced hand with a long club suit. Once responder bypasses hearts and spades and fails to support diamonds, his 13 cards invariably include at least four clubs. **A 1NT response to 1◇ is almost the equivalent of a club *bid*.**

As for HCP, "everyone" agrees that this 1NT response promises 6-10 HCP.

You open 1◇ and partner responds 1NT. Now what?

1. ♠ A 7 5 3   ♡ K Q 8   ◇ J 6 5 4 2   ♣ A

2. ♠ A K   ♡ A 4   ◇ J 6 5 4 2   ♣ 5 4 3 2

3. ♠ A Q   ♡ K J   ◇ K 7 6 5 3 2   ♣ K 7 4

4. ♠ 6 4   ♡ A K J   ◇ A Q 7 5 4 3   ♣ K 4

5. ♠ Q 7 5 4   ♡ A K Q   ◇ K 8 7 5 3   ♣ K

6. ♠ A   ♡ K 8 7   ◇ A Q J 4 2   ♣ A Q 6 4

7. ♠ 6 4 3   ♡ A 9   ◇ A K Q J 9 7   ♣ 8 4

8. ♠ K Q   ♡ K Q 10   ◇ K Q J 8 6 2   ♣ J 3

9. ♠ A 3   ♡ A 8   ◇ A J 10 9 6 4   ♣ A 6 2

Opener Rebids after 1♢ – 1NT

1.   ♠ A 7 5 3   ♡ K Q 8   ♢ J 6 5 4 2   ♣ A

Pass. Because partner could be holding five or six clubs with fewer than three diamonds, you don't really want to insist on diamonds as trumps. In addition, once partner promised clubs with his 1NT response, your singleton ace became less of a liability for notrump.

When all is said and done, I would remain at the one level, hoping that partner is able to scrape up seven tricks.

2.   ♠ A K   ♡ A 4   ♢ J 6 5 4 2   ♣ 5 4 3 2

Bid 2♣. Once partner denies four cards in either major, your side has a 100% guarantee of a minor-suit fit (or two). Although you do have major-suit stoppers, you have an unbalanced hand. Your two doubletons will be assets in a suit contract, but not in notrump.

3.   ♠ A Q   ♡ K J   ♢ K 7 6 5 3 2   ♣ K 7 4

Bid 2♢. Your 16 HCP suggest making a stronger bid, but with a weak long suit and only one ace, you should prefer to stay low. Keep in mind that your hand would be the dummy in a notrump contract, and the opening lead will come *through* you. For that reason, I like to open 1NT with hands like this to ensure declaring in notrump.

4.   ♠ 6 4   ♡ A K J   ♢ A Q 7 5 4 3   ♣ K 4

Bid 2♡, not 3♢. The reverse into hearts with only three cards is necessary to let partner know you've got *that* major covered, along with a strong hand containing at least five diamonds.

5. ♠ Q 7 5 4 ♡ A K Q ◇ K 8 7 5 3 ♣ K

Bid 2NT, not 2♠. Despite your unbalanced distribution, there is no reason to avoid notrump with this hand. The invitational raise accurately describes your 17 HCP. Since partner denied spades, your weak major is not worth talking about. You are well-prepared for a lead in your shorter major, and partner usually has club length and strength for a 1NT response to 1◇.

6. ♠ A ♡ K 8 7 ◇ A Q J 4 2 ♣ A Q 6 4

Bid 3♣. A club slam is a distinct possibility. After forcing to game, you hope that your side will be able to decide whether to play in clubs, diamonds or notrump.

7. ♠ 6 4 3 ♡ A 9 ◇ A K Q J 9 7 ♣ 8 4

Bid 2NT, not 3◇, and certainly not 2◇! This is a perfect hand to invite 3NT. In addition, if responder has a minimum with only one winner, it will be easier to take *eight* tricks in notrump rather than *nine* tricks in diamonds.

8. ♠ K Q ♡ K Q 10 ◇ K Q J 8 6 2 ♣ J 3

Bid 3◇, not 2NT. You need time to knock out their aces; so if partner is unable to accept your invitation, a diamond part-score will be safer than playing in 2NT.

9. ♠ A 3 ♡ A 8 ◇ A J 10 9 6 4 ♣ A 6 2

Bid 3NT. You should be happy to insist on game with this VERY upgradable hand. Four aces and a 6-card suit loaded with intermediate cards — who could ask for anything more?

Sometimes, Seven is Enough

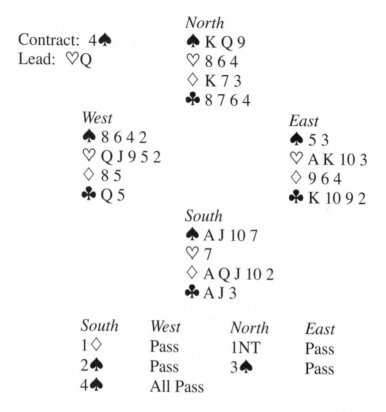

Contract: 4♠
Lead: ♡Q

North
♠ K Q 9
♡ 8 6 4
◇ K 7 3
♣ 8 7 6 4

West
♠ 8 6 4 2
♡ Q J 9 5 2
◇ 8 5
♣ Q 5

East
♠ 5 3
♡ A K 10 3
◇ 9 6 4
♣ K 10 9 2

South
♠ A J 10 7
♡ 7
◇ A Q J 10 2
♣ A J 3

South	West	North	East
1◇	Pass	1NT	Pass
2♠	Pass	3♠	Pass
4♠	All Pass		

At her second turn, South reversed into spades to show her second suit and strong, unbalanced hand. North's 1NT response had denied a 4-card major. With that in mind, his support for spades was excellent — so he raised to 3♠.

South realized that her partner had only three spades, but with three spade honors, she was willing to play the 4-3 fit.

The defense persisted with hearts. If South had ruffed in, she couldn't have handled the 4-2 spade split. Instead, she discarded clubs on the second and third round of hearts. She could then win the club shift, draw trumps, and claim.

Chapter 9

Opener Rebids after 1♡ – 1NT

A traditional 1NT response to a major shows 6-10 HCP, and denies 3-card support for opener's suit. However, one of the most popular of the modern conventions is 1NT Forcing. As long as the opponents are silent, opener will NEVER pass a 1NT response after opening 1♡ or 1♠ in first or second seat. Responder might have only 5 HCP, but could have as many as 12. Also, responder could have 3-card support, although this is rare.

I wanted to make this book applicable for everyone. Therefore, all of the examples in chapters 9 and 10 were constructed so that the answer will be the same regardless of your partnership agreements.

You open 1♡ and partner responds 1NT. Whether or not you play "1NT Forcing," what's your bid?

1. ♠ 4 3 ♡ A J 10 9 6 ◇ 5 3 ♣ K Q J 9
2. ♠ 4 ♡ A K J 7 6 ◇ A K Q ♣ 5 4 3 2
3. ♠ A 7 ♡ A 8 7 6 5 2 ◇ A Q 10 9 ♣ 3
4. ♠ K Q J 7 ♡ K Q J 10 8 ◇ 5 4 2 ♣ 3
5. ♠ Q J 4 2 ♡ K J 9 8 5 4 ◇ A ♣ K Q
6. ♠ A K J 9 ♡ A Q J 6 5 2 ◇ 8 ♣ 5 4
7. ♠ K Q J ♡ K 7 6 5 3 ◇ K J 3 ♣ A J
8. ♠ A K 6 ♡ A Q J 10 3 ◇ A 10 3 ♣ 7 4
9. ♠ A 4 ♡ A K 10 9 2 ◇ 9 ♣ K Q J 10 4
10. ♠ Q J 8 2 ♡ A K 6 5 3 ◇ K Q ♣ A J
11. ♠ A 3 ♡ Q J 10 9 6 5 3 ◇ K Q J 9 ♣ —

1.   ♠ 4 3   ♥ A J 10 9 6   ◇ 5 3   ♣ K Q J 9
Bid 2♣. This bid is automatic for 1NT Forcing players, but also correct for "standard" players. With two strong suits, this hand should play well in either clubs or hearts.

2.   ♠ 4   ♥ A K J 7 6   ◇ A K Q   ♣ 5 4 3 2
Bid an imperfect 2♣. Partner will not know that your clubs are lousy or that you have a 17-count; however, all alternatives are even less appealing. **When in doubt, make the cheapest reasonable bid.**

3.   ♠ A 7   ♥ A 8 7 6 5 2   ◇ A Q 10 9   ♣ 3
Bid 2◇. Your strong diamonds, weak hearts and promising hand all argue for 2◇ rather than 2♥. Most 6-4 hands shouldn't leave their 4-card suit on the shelf – especially when the suit sparkles.

4.   ♠ K Q J 7   ♥ K Q J 10 8   ◇ 5 4 2   ♣ 3
Bid 2♥. Even if partner has a singleton heart, 2♥ should be a sensible partscore. **Great suits don't have to follow normal guidelines.**

5.   ♠ Q J 4 2   ♥ K J 9 8 5 4   ◇ A   ♣ K Q
Bid 2♥, not 2♠. With two mediocre suits, and 9 HCP squished into your short suits, this hand is not worth a stronger bid.

6.   ♠ A K J 9   ♥ A Q J 6 5 2   ◇ 8   ♣ 5 4
Bid 2♠. With two excellent suits, you are happy to reverse despite only 15 HCP. At your next turn, you'll rebid hearts.

7. ♠ K Q J ♡ K 7 6 5 3 ◇ K J 3 ♣ A J

Bid 2NT. This is a very overrated 18-count. You have too many jacks and not enough aces. You have "only" three quick tricks, which is a very low number for a hand with 18 HCP. You're also not crazy about your very weak long suit and lack of intermediate cards. If partner passes 2NT, you will have no regrets.

8. ♠ A K 6 ♡ A Q J 10 3 ◇ A 10 3 ♣ 7 4

Bid 3NT, not 2NT. The distribution and 18 HCP are the same as the previous hand, but that's where the similarity ends. This beauty features 4½ quick tricks, a pair of promising tens, and a heart suit that will definitely provide a source of tricks.

9. ♠ A 4 ♡ A K 10 9 2 ◇ 9 ♣ K Q J 10 4

Bid 3♣. Only 17 HCP, but with your tremendous playing strength, you're happy to force to game. If partner has club support and two useful cards, slam is quite possible.

10. ♠ Q J 8 2 ♡ A K 6 5 3 ◇ K Q ♣ A J

Bid 3NT, not 2♠. With such strong doubletons, there is no reason to avoid notrump, and partner's 1NT response did deny four spades. A spade bid would only serve to help the opponents select an opening lead.

11. ♠ A 3 ♡ Q J 10 9 6 5 3 ◇ K Q J 9 ♣ —

Bid 4♡. With hearts as trump, you expect to win five heart tricks, three diamonds, and the ♠A. Even if partner has only one useful high card, you have excellent chances of scoring this up.

Not the Obvious Finesse

Contract: 4♡
Lead: ◇K

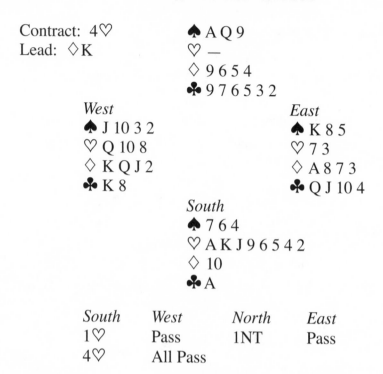

```
                    ♠ A Q 9
                    ♡ —
                    ◇ 9 6 5 4
                    ♣ 9 7 6 5 3 2
    West                            East
    ♠ J 10 3 2                      ♠ K 8 5
    ♡ Q 10 8                        ♡ 7 3
    ◇ K Q J 2                       ◇ A 8 7 3
    ♣ K 8                           ♣ Q J 10 4
                    South
                    ♠ 7 6 4
                    ♡ A K J 9 6 5 4 2
                    ◇ 10
                    ♣ A
```

South	West	North	East
1♡	Pass	1NT	Pass
4♡	All Pass		

South was too strong to open 4♡, but lost no time jumping to game once North responded.

Declarer ruffed the second diamond, and cashed the ace and king of hearts. When the ♡Q didn't drop, the contract seemed to depend on the location of the ♠K.

Fortunately, South appreciated *all* of dummy's spades, and led a spade to the nine. When this forced out the king, the only remaining loser was the ♡Q. If the ♠9 had lost to the ten or jack, declarer could still finesse the ♠Q.

It wouldn't matter if West had played an honor when spades were first led. South could cover with the ♠Q and finesse the ♠9 later on.

Chapter 10

Opener Rebids after 1♠ – 1NT

Everything here mirrors what was said earlier about a 1NT response to a 1♡ opening bid.

One additional note about 1♠ – 1NT. A 1NT response to 1♡ denies spades, because responder could *easily* bid the suit at the one level with four spades and six points. On the other hand, a 2-level response in a major requires additional strength and at least five cards; so, in any system, a 1NT response to 1♠ *may* contain a weak hand with a long heart suit. When faced with a close decision, opener should prefer a cheaper bid, just in case responder has a heart suit he'd like to talk about.

You open 1♠ and partner responds 1NT. Whether or not you play "1NT Forcing," what's your bid?

1.   ♠ A 8 7 6 3 2   ♡ A K 10   ◇ —   ♣ A 7 5 2

2.   ♠ K Q J 9 6 5   ♡ A 5 3   ◇ —   ♣ J 7 5 2

3.   ♠ A K J 10 5   ♡ —   ◇ K Q J 8   ♣ 7 6 5 3

4.   ♠ Q J 5 4 3   ♡ K J   ◇ A K 6 5 3   ♣ A

5.   ♠ A K J 8 7   ♡ 10 8 5 3   ◇ A K J 9   ♣ —

6.   ♠ A K 10 6 5 2   ♡ 6   ◇ A Q 7   ♣ A K 8

7.   ♠ A K 10 9 8   ♡ A K J 10 9   ◇ —   ♣ 7 6 3

8.   ♠ K J 10 9 8 4 2   ♡ A K J   ◇ 7   ♣ 6 2

Opener Rebids after 1♠ – 1NT

1.   ♠ A 8 7 6 3 2   ♡ A K 10   ◇ —   ♣ A 7 5 2

Bid 2♣ with this flexible hand. Your best fit could be in clubs or even hearts. The economical 2♣ bid gives you the best chance to find a fit, and does not rule out playing in spades if partner has more than one.

Although your spade suit is weak, this is a very upgradable hand. You have four quick tricks and superb distribution. In fact, if partner has length in clubs or hearts, even a slam is possible.

2.   ♠ K Q J 9 6 5   ♡ A 5 3   ◇ —   ♣ J 7 5 2

Bid 2♠, not 2♣. Same distribution as the previous hand, but your great spades and minimum hand suggest that you should be content to try for a spade part-score.

3.   ♠ A K J 10 5   ♡ —   ◇ K Q J 8   ♣ 7 6 5 3

Bid 2◇. When you have two 4-card minors, you might as well bid your stronger suit. If partner has a long heart suit and bids 2♡, you will retreat to 2♠ and hope to survive.

4.   ♠ Q J 5 4 3   ♡ K J   ◇ A K 6 5 3   ♣ A

Bid 2◇. A very nice hand, but you are a tad short of a game-forcing jump-shift.

What would make this hand strong enough to allow you to force to game? You would be better off if your heart and club honors could "relocate" in either of your long suits. Of course, as long as you are "wishing upon a star," you'd also be grateful if your two long suits were bolstered by the addition of a few intermediates.

5.   ♠ A K J 8 7   ♡ 10 8 5 3   ◇ A K J 9   ♣ —
Bid 2♡. Although your diamonds are more impressive than your hearts, you must seize this opportunity to show your 4-card major. If partner takes a preference to spades, you'll bid 3◇ (encouraging, but not forcing).

6.   ♠ A K 10 6 5 2   ♡ 6   ◇ A Q 7   ♣ A K 8
Bid 3♣. Forcing to game is obvious, but you have no idea which game (or possibly slam) you belong in. If you don't like the jump-shift into a 3-card suit — neither do I. Sometimes, it's unavoidable, but this one could have been avoided by opening 2♣. **With a long major suit and a great hand, don't hesitate to open 2♣.**

7.   ♠ A K 10 9 8   ♡ A K J 10 9   ◇ —   ♣ 7 6 3
Bid 3♡. Forcing to game with 15 HCP after a 1-level response is very unusual. However, because you need so little to make 4♡, if you bid 2♡ and everyone passed, you might miss a laydown game. If your second suit were a minor, you would be content to bid only two, and you'd be less concerned about possibly missing an 11-trick game.

If partner now bids 3♠ or 3NT, you'll continue with 4♡, hoping that partner has three hearts. Of course, with your superb intermediates, even if partner has a doubleton, you might be able to bring home a major-suit game.

8.   ♠ K J 10 9 8 4 2   ♡ A K J   ◇ 7   ♣ 6 2
Bid 3♠ to invite game. With prospects of eight tricks in your own hand, you have too much offense to bid only 2♠. If partner now bids 3NT, you will bid 4♠ based on your independent suit.

The *Almost* Killing Lead

Contract: 4♡
Lead: ♡2

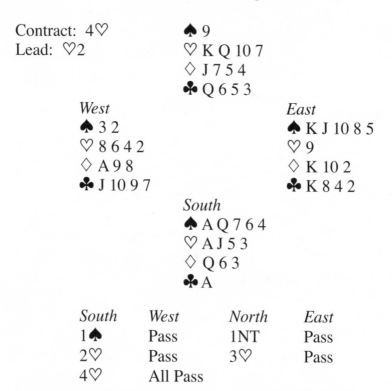

```
                    ♠ 9
                    ♡ K Q 10 7
                    ◇ J 7 5 4
                    ♣ Q 6 5 3
West                                East
♠ 3 2                               ♠ K J 10 8 5
♡ 8 6 4 2                           ♡ 9
◇ A 9 8                             ◇ K 10 2
♣ J 10 9 7                          ♣ K 8 4 2
                    South
                    ♠ A Q 7 6 4
                    ♡ A J 5 3
                    ◇ Q 6 3
                    ♣ A
```

South	West	North	East
1♠	Pass	1NT	Pass
2♡	Pass	3♡	Pass
4♡	All Pass		

South had a nice hand, but was not strong enough to jump-shift. North was glad to "support with support," and South had an easy 4♡ bid.

90 out of 100 players would have cheerfully led the ♣J. Declarer could win the ♣A, cash the ♠A, and crossruff each of her side's eight trumps. Once dummy denied spades, however, West made the excellent lead of a trump.

South won the ♡K, which left only six trumps to crossruff. She needed another winner, so led a spade to the ♠Q and said her prayers. When the finesse won, she cashed her black aces. Having won four tricks, she happily crossruffed her six remaining trumps.

Rebidding after Opening in 3rd or 4th Seat

Opener usually makes the same rebid as he would if his partner was not a passed hand. In addition, the meaning of his bid does not change. However, when selecting his rebid, opener must keep the following in mind:

1. Partner's response in a new suit is no longer forcing. Therefore, opener is free to pass with a minimum opening bid or a hand where he opened light. Of course, he should pass only when game is out of the question AND the partnership is in a playable contract.

South	West	North	East
Pass	Pass	1♣	Pass
1♡	Pass	???	

♠ J 5 ♡ 6 4 3 ♢ A K ♣ A 9 7 6 4 3

Pass. Opposite an unpassed hand, you would have rebid 2♣, but once partner passed, 1♡ is high enough.

♠ 8 7 5 ♡ A ♢ K 8 4 ♣ K 8 7 6 4 3

Bid 2♣. You wouldn't have opened this hand in 1st or 2nd seat, but you can't leave partner in 1♡ with a singleton.

2. Slam is very unlikely, so opener should be practical.

South	West	North	East
Pass	Pass	1♢	Pass
1♠	Pass	???	

♠ J 10 9 6 ♡ Q ♢ A K Q J ♣ K Q J 9

Bid 4♠. If partner was an unpassed hand, you'd try for slam with a 4♡ splinter bid. Since he couldn't open, you're not interested.

Opener's Advanced Rebids:
Not for the Faint of Heart

Jump Reverse –   **ALERT**
after a response in a major

1♣ – 1♡
3♢   ♠ A Q J   ♡ K Q 7 5   ♢ 7   ♣ K 8 6 4 2

A 2♢ reverse would be forcing, showing a real diamond
suit. Therefore, jumping to 3♢ to show 19-20 HCP is
unnecessary because it wastes so much bidding space.

Accordingly, some experienced players define a jump
reverse as a "mini-splinter" with 4-card support for
responder's major. Opener is inviting game with 17-18
distributional points, as well as showing 0-1 cards in the
new "suit." This information will allow responder to
evaluate his cards more accurately. He can jump to game,
but is also welcome to sign off in 3♡ or try for slam.

Jump Reverse –   **ALERT**
after a 1NT response

1♢ – 1NT
3♡   ♠ A 8 7   ♡ 8   ♢ A K Q 10 7 4   ♣ A J 2

Once again, because opener's reverse (2♡) would be
forcing, the jump reverse makes no sense as a natural bid.
Opener's jump is a splinter bid, promising a 6-card suit and
a *very* strong hand along with shortness in the suit bid.
Responder can bid 3NT with heart strength. Otherwise, he
will jump to 5♢, sign off in 4♢, or even introduce a long
club suit.

4 of Opener's Minor
after a response in a major

NO ALERT
(explain after auction)

1♣ – 1♠

4♣   ♠ K Q 10 5   ♡ A   ◇ 7 5   ♣ K Q 9 7 6 4

The double jump to four of opener's minor shows 4-card support for responder's major, and a very strong 6-card suit. Because of the great distribution, opener does not need as many HCP as he would for a splinter bid.

Bidding a strong 3-card suit when stuck

NO ALERT

1♣ – 1♡

1♠   ♠ A K J   ♡ A 8 5   ◇ A   ♣ J 7 6 4 3 2

Because opener is lying about the length of his suit, and his bid in a new suit is not forcing, there are risks involved. However, the bid is economical and responder rarely passes; therefore it gives you the best chance to cope with an otherwise "unbiddable" hand. Once you hear a second bid from responder, you will be better-placed.

3-Card Club "Support" after 1◇ – 1NT

NO ALERT

1◇ – 1NT

2♣   ♠ A 8 7 5   ♡ 4   ◇ 8 7 5 4 2   ♣ A K J

With a major-suit singleton, opener is desperate to escape from 1NT. When partner responds 1NT to 1◇, he virtually guarantees four or more clubs, but he might also be short in diamonds. With your three strong clubs and five atrocious diamonds, bidding 2♣ is far more flexible than 2◇. If responder prefers diamonds, he can take you back to 2◇.

Hardcover Books by Marty Bergen

More Declarer Play the Bergen Way How to Make More Contracts	$18.95
Declarer Play the Bergen Way 2005 Bridge Book of the year!	$18.95
Bergen for the Defense Sharpen Your Defensive Skills	$18.95
MARTY SEZ... Volume 1 Bergen's Bevy of Bridge Secrets	$17.95
MARTY SEZ... Volume 2 More Secrets of Winning Bridge	$17.95
MARTY SEZ... Volume 3 Practical Tips You Can Take to the Bank	$17.95
POINTS SCHMOINTS! Alltime Bestseller and Bridge Book of the Year	$19.95
More POINTS SCHMOINTS! Sequel to the Award-Winning Bestseller	$19.95
Better Bidding with Bergen, Vol. 1 Improve your constructive bidding	$16.95
Better Bidding with Bergen, Vol. 2 Improve your competetive bidding	$14.95
Schlemiel...Schlimazel? Mensch! (nonbridge) An Entertaining Guide to Becoming the Best You can be	$14.95

•• VERY SPECIAL OFFER ••

Buy one of these hardcover books from Marty
and receive a **free** copy of any one
of his eight softcover books.
Buy 2 hardcovers and get 3 free softcover books (page 72)
Personalized autographs available upon request.

Interactive CDs for the Computer

Guaranteed to improve your game. Great graphics!
All software originated with Fred Gitelman,
"the Bill Gates of bridge software."

by Marty Bergen

POINTS SCHMOINTS!	~~$29.95~~	$25
Marty Sez...	~~$24.95~~	$20

Very Special Offer! Get both CDs for $30
For free demos of Bergen CDs, e-mail Marty at:
mbergen@mindspring.com

**Mention this book and get a free Bergen softcover
(choice of 8) with each Lawrence or Gitelman CD!**

Five CDs by Mike Lawrence

Conventions, Defense, 2/1, Private Lessons 1 and 2 (declarer play). Marty's discount price is $30 each. (Conventions is $35)

by Fred Gitelman

Bridge Master 2000	~~$59.95~~	$48

"Best software ever created for improving your declarer play."

by Kit Woolsey

Cavendish 2000:		
Day 1, Days 2-3	~~$29.95~~	$19 each

by Larry Cohen

Free demos available at: larryco.com/index.html

Play Bridge With Larry Cohen
"One of the best products to come along in years. Easy-to-use. Suitable for all players..."

Special Sale!!

Day 1	voted best software 2002	~~$29.95~~	$19
Day 2, Day 3		~~$29.95~~	$19
My Favorite 52	best software 2005	~~$29.95~~	$19

Softcover Books by Marty Bergen
Buy 2, then get 1 (equal or lesser price) for half price!

Bergen's Best Bridge Tips	$7.95
Bergen's Best Bridge Quizzes, Vol. 1	$7.95
To Open or Not to Open	$6.95
Better Rebidding with Bergen	$7.95
Understanding 1NT Forcing	$5.95
Hand Evaluation: Points, Schmoints!	$7.95
Introduction to Negative Doubles	$6.95
Negative Doubles	$9.95

The Official Encyclopedia of Bridge
(more than 800 pages)

Highlights include extensive sections on: suit combinations, explanation of all conventions, techniques for bidding, defense, leads, declarer play, and a complete glossary of bridge terms.

The encyclopedia retails for $39.95
Marty's price: $23 + shipping plus 1 free softcover book!

• ORDERING INFORMATION •

To place your order, call Marty toll-free at:
1-800-386-7432
All major credit cards are welcome
Or send a check or money order (U.S. funds) to:

Marty Bergen
9 River Chase Terrace
Palm Beach Gardens, FL 33418-6817

If ordering by mail, please call or email for S&H details.